America–
Still Unprepared,
Still in Danger

*Report of an Independent Task Force
Sponsored by the
Council on Foreign Relations*

Gary Hart and Warren B. Rudman,
Co-Chairs
Stephen E. Flynn,
Project Director

TASK FORCE MEMBERS

CHARLES G. BOYD

WARREN CHRISTOPHER

WILLIAM J. CROWE

STEPHEN E. FLYNN

STEPHEN FRIEDMAN

GARY HART

JAMES K. KALLSTROM

JOSHUA LEDERBERG

DONALD B. MARRON

PHILIP A. ODEEN

WARREN B. RUDMAN

GEORGE P. SHULTZ

ANNE-MARIE SLAUGHTER

HAROLD E. VARMUS

JOHN W. VESSEY

WILLIAM H. WEBSTER

STEVEN WEINBERG

CONTENTS

FOREWORD

Attacks against Americans on U.S. soil that may involve weapons of mass destruction are likely, but the structures and strategies to respond to this serious threat are fragmented and inadequate. So warned the U.S. Commission on National Security led by former senators Gary Hart and Warren B. Rudman in their final report released on March 15, 2001. Hardly anyone in Washington or the mainstream media paid any attention. They should not make the same mistake twice by overlooking the key finding from the report of this Task Force, again co-chaired by Senators Hart and Rudman: "A year after September 11, America remains dangerously unprepared to prevent and respond to a catastrophic terrorist attack on U.S. soil."

This chilling conclusion comes on the eve of what now appears to be a pending war with Iraq to dethrone Saddam Hussein. It was arrived at by a bipartisan group that includes two former secretaries of state, three Nobel laureates, two former chairmen of the Joint Chiefs of Staff, a former director of the Central Intelligence Agency (CIA) and the Federal Bureau of Investigation (FBI), and some of the nation's most distinguished financial, legal, and medical authorities. Of the dozens of Independent Task Forces that have been assembled during my decade-long tenure as president of the Council on Foreign Relations, no report has been so timely or important.

Around the anniversary of September 11, we were saturated with one-year retrospectives. If there are Americans on Main Street or in the halls of government who have concluded that it is now time to get back to our "normal" lives, this report is mandatory reading. As the Task Force participants conclude, we are entering a time of especially grave danger. We are preparing to attack a ruthless adversary who may well have access to weapons of mass destruction. Yet we will not see the full effect of many of the post–September 11 initiatives undertaken by the president, Congress, governors, and mayors for some time. This is no one's fault. It simply reflects the fact that you cannot turn a nation as large and complex as this one on a dime.

Still, given the stakes—potentially the loss of thousands of innocent American lives and the mass disruption of America's economy and society—there are things we must be doing on an emergency basis to reduce our vulnerabilities here at home. Let me stress that the Task Force report does all this without thinking about or placing political blame for what has not been done to prepare our nation against terror attacks. The Task Force was dedicated to creating a necessary sense of urgency and to helping get the necessary things done. This Task Force lays out a series of recommendations that should help guide the nation's efforts in the weeks and months ahead.

My deepest appreciation and admiration go to Senators Rudman and Hart for agreeing to lead this Task Force. The Council and the nation owe a debt to them and all the other distinguished Task Force members who brought their vast and diverse professional expertise to this enterprise. They selflessly agreed to serve on very short notice to prepare this report with the same sense of urgency that our current circumstances clearly warrant. On a personal note, having served with the two formidable former senators on their National Security Commission, I can think of no more qualified people to take on this responsibility. My thanks also go to Council Senior Fellow Stephen E. Flynn, who served as project director, lending his considerable expertise, draftsmanship, and independence of thought to crafting and informing what follows. He was very ably assisted by the Council's Army military fellow, Colonel (P) Sal Cambria, and research associates Rob Knake and Uday Ram.

This Task Force has made an outstanding contribution to informing how we should proceed in the post–September 11 security environment. Shame on us if we do not pay heed to both the warning and the wisdom of what is outlined on the pages that follow.

Leslie H. Gelb
President
Council on Foreign Relations

ACKNOWLEDGMENTS

When Les Gelb approached me in late July with the proposal that I serve as project director for an Independent Task Force on Homeland Security Imperatives, I voiced some trepidation. His aim was for the Task Force to operate essentially on a wartime footing—something our home front rightfully should be on, given the likelihood of a second catastrophic terrorist attack more deadly and disruptive than what we suffered on September 11, 2001. I wondered aloud if we could assemble a blue-ribbon Task Force with just a couple of weeks' notice and demand so much of its members' time and energy in the following sixty-day period. As soon as he told me that Senator Warren Rudman and Senator Gary Hart had agreed to co-chair the Task Force, my doubts evaporated. I had the privilege to serve with them while they were at the helm of the now famous Hart-Rudman U.S. Commission on National Security. There could be no better chairs for this initiative, as events over the ensuing weeks proved. I count it as a highlight of my professional career to have again been afforded the opportunity to work with them.

I have drawn added inspiration from the generosity of intellect, wisdom, and time of all our distinguished Task Force members. What a special experience it has been to be a part of an enterprise with these most extraordinary Americans. Secretary George Shultz, Secretary Warren Christopher, General John Vessey, Admiral William Crowe, General Charles Boyd, Judge William Webster, Dr. Joshua Lederberg, Dr. Harold Varmus, Dr. Steven Weinberg, Dean Anne-Marie Slaughter, Mr. Philip Odeen, Mr. Donald Marron, Mr. Stephen Friedman, and Mr. James Kallstrom—thank you for your grace and responsiveness in the face of draconian deadlines, and a steady stream of late night e-mails, faxes, and phone calls.

My debt to Les Gelb extends beyond his affording me the opportunity to serve as project director—he also made every possible

Council resource available to support me. He was instrumental in sharpening the focus, structure, and language of the initial concept paper that got us launched. Most important, he assigned my colleague, Colonel (P) Sal Cambria, to serve as the Task Force coordinator. Colonel (P) Cambria has flawlessly tended to the innumerable details to get the Task Force from its starting point to the finish line. Finally, I have received extraordinary research support from two of the Council's brightest and most energetic research associates, Rob Knake and Uday Ram. In short, if this Task Force report misses the mark in contributing substantively to the national conversation on this vital issue, the responsibility lies completely with me, since no project director has been afforded more ingredients for potential success. And, underpinning all of the above, I am grateful for the Arthur Ross Foundation's support of Task Forces that gave us the ability to move forward as swiftly as the urgency of the issues demanded.

Stephen E. Flynn
Project Director

EXECUTIVE SUMMARY

When you see the multiple attacks that you've seen occur around the world, from Bali to Kuwait, the number of failed attacks that have been attempted, the various messages that have been issued by senior al-Qaeda leaders, you must make the assumption that al-Qaeda is in an execution phase and intends to strike us both here and overseas; that's unambiguous as far as I am concerned.

—George Tenet, Director of Central Intelligence,
Testimony before the Senate Select Committee on Intelligence,
October 17, 2002

A year after September 11, 2001, America remains dangerously unprepared to prevent and respond to a catastrophic terrorist attack on U.S. soil. In all likelihood, the next attack will result in even greater casualties and widespread disruption to American lives and the economy. The need for immediate action is made more urgent by the prospect of the United States's going to war with Iraq and the possibility that Saddam Hussein might threaten the use of weapons of mass destruction (WMD) in America.

The Task Force recognizes that important and generally salutary measures have been undertaken since September 11 to respond to the risk of catastrophic terrorism, including pending legislation to create the Department of Homeland Security, which should be enacted on an urgent basis. Yet, there is still cause for concern. After a year without a new attack, there are already signs that Americans are lapsing back into complacency. Also, a war with Iraq could consume virtually all the nation's attention and command the bulk of the available resources. President George W. Bush has declared that combating terrorism requires a war on two fronts—at home and abroad. The Task Force believes the nation should respond accordingly. It outlines a number of homeland security priorities that should be pursued with the same sense of urgency and national purpose as our overseas exertions.

Among the risks that the United States still confronts are the following:

- Some 650,000 local and state police officials continue to operate in a virtual intelligence vacuum, without access to terrorist watch lists provided by the U.S. Department of State to immigration and consular officials.

- While 50,000 federal screeners are being hired at the nation's airports to check passengers, only the tiniest percentage of containers, ships, trucks, and trains that enter the United States each day are subject to examination—and a weapon of mass destruction could well be hidden among this cargo. Should the maritime or surface elements of America's global transportation system be used as a weapon-delivery device, the response right now would almost certainly be to shut the system down at an enormous cost to the economies of the United States and its trade partners.

- First responders—police, fire, and emergency medical personnel—are not prepared for a chemical or biological attack. Their radios cannot communicate with one another, and they lack the training and gear to protect themselves and the public in an emergency. The consequence of this could be the unnecessary loss of thousands of American lives.

- America's own ill-prepared response could hurt its people to a much greater extent than any single attack by a terrorist. America is a powerful and resilient nation, and terrorists are not supermen. But the risk of self-inflicted harm to America's liberties and way of life is greatest during and immediately following a national trauma.

- An adversary intent on disrupting America's reliance on energy need not target oil fields in the Middle East. The homeland infrastructure for refining and distributing energy to support the daily lives of Americans remains largely unprotected from sabotage.

- While the overwhelming majority of the nation's critical infrastructure is owned and operated by the private sector, significant legal barriers remain to forging effective private-public partnerships on homeland security issues. These include potential antitrust conflicts, concerns about the public release of sensitive security information by way of the Freedom of Information Act (FOIA), and liability exposure.

- Domestic security measures must be pursued within an international context. The critical infrastructures that support the daily lives of Americans are linked to global networks. Efforts to protect these systems will fail unless they are pursued abroad as well as at home.

- The National Guard is currently equipped and trained primarily for carrying out its role in supporting conventional combat units overseas. The homeland security mission can draw on many of these capabilities but it requires added emphasis on bolstering the capacity of National Guard units to respond to biological attacks; acquiring protection, detection, and other equipment that is tailored for complex urban environments; and special training to provide civil support in the aftermath of a large-scale catastrophic attack.

Key Recommendations

- Empower front-line agents to intercept terrorists by establishing a twenty-four-hour operations center in each state that can provide access to terrorist watch list information via real time intergovernmental links between local and federal law enforcement agencies.

- Make first responders ready to respond by immediately providing federal funds to clear the backlog of requests for protective gear, training, and communications equipment. State and local budgets cannot bankroll these necessities in the near term.

- Recalibrate the agenda for transportation security; the vulnerabilities are greater and the stakes are higher in the sea and land modes than in commercial aviation. Systems such as those used in the aviation sector, which start from the assumption that every passenger and every bag of luggage poses an equal risk, must give way to more intelligence-driven and layered security approaches that emphasize prescreening and monitoring based on risk criteria.

- Fund energy distribution vulnerability assessments to be completed in no more than six months, fund a stockpile of modular backup components to quickly restore the operation of the energy grid should it be targeted, and work with Canada to put in place adequate security measures for cross-border pipelines.
- Strengthen the capacity of local, state, and federal public heath and agricultural agencies to detect and conduct disease-outbreak investigations. The key to mitigating casualties associated with a biological attack against people or the food supply is to identify the source of infection as early as possible.
- Enact an "Omnibus Anti–Red Tape" law with a two-year sunset clause for approved private-public homeland security task forces to include (1) a fast-track security clearance process that permits the sharing of "secret-level" classified information with non-federal and industry leaders; (2) an FOIA exemption in instances when leaders in critical infrastructure industries agree to share information about their security vulnerabilities with federal agencies; (3) an exemption of private participants in these task forces from antitrust rules; (4) homeland security appropriations to be managed under the more liberal rules governing research and development programs in the Department of Defense rather than the normal federal acquisition rules; and (5) liability safeguards and limits.
- Fund, equip, and train National Guard units around the country to ensure they can support the new state homeland security plans under development by each governor. Also, triple the number of National Guard WMD Civil Support Teams from twenty-two to sixty-six.

Quickly mobilizing the nation to prepare for the worst is an act of prudence, not fatalism. In the twenty-first century, security and liberty are inseparable. The absence of adequate security elevates the risk that laws passed immediately in the wake of surprise terrorist attacks will be reactive, not deliberative. Predictably, the consequence will be to compound the initial harm incurred by a tragic event with measures that overreach in terms of imposing costly new security mandates and the assumption of new government authorities that may erode our freedoms. Accordingly, aggressively pursuing America's homeland security imperatives quickly and immediately may well be the most important thing we can do to sustain America's cherished freedoms for future generations.

Preparedness at home plays a critical role in combating terrorism by reducing its appeal as an effective means of warfare. Acts of catastrophic terrorism produce not only deaths and physical destruction but also societal and economic disruption. Thus, as important as it is to try and attack terrorist organizations overseas and isolate those who support them, it is equally important to eliminate the incentive for undertaking these acts in the first place. If the disruptive effects of terrorism can be sharply reduced, if not eliminated, America's adversaries may be deterred from taking their battles to the streets of the American homeland.

TASK FORCE REPORT

INTRODUCTION

A year after September 11, 2001, America remains dangerously unprepared to prevent and respond to a catastrophic terrorist attack on U.S. soil. In all likelihood, the next attack will result in even greater casualties and widespread disruption to American lives and the economy. The need for immediate action is made more urgent by the prospect of the United States's going to war with Iraq and the possibility that Saddam Hussein might threaten the use of weapons of mass destruction (WMD) in America.

This report's recommendations are intended to focus the nation on what must be done on an emergency basis to prevent attacks and to limit the consequences of these attacks should U.S. prevention efforts fail. The Bush administration, Congress, governors, and mayors around the country have taken important measures since September 11 to respond to the risk of catastrophic terrorism. Legislation creating the Department of Homeland Security should be enacted on an urgent basis, and initiatives to improve U.S. intelligence operations must go forward. But the United States will not see the full effect of these fundamental changes for several years. In the meantime Americans cannot afford to become complacent. Our enemies are not idle.

The Task Force identified six critical mandates that deserve the nation's immediate attention:

- Empower front-line agents to prevent terrorist attacks and make first responders ready to respond; 650,000 local and state law enforcement officers are operating in a counterterrorism information vacuum, and first responders are not nearly ready enough to respond to catastrophic events.
- Make trade security a global priority; the system for moving goods affordably and reliably around the world is ripe for exploitation and vulnerable to mass disruption by terrorists.

- Set critical infrastructure-protection priorities; some potential targets pose a graver risk for mass disruption than others.
- Enhance America's public health system so that it is able to quickly detect and respond to biological attacks.
- Move quickly to clear federal obstacles to forging effective private-public security partnerships by addressing industry concerns with respect to potential antitrust conflicts, public release of sensitive security information by way of the Freedom of Information Act (FOIA), and liability exposure.
- Fund, train, and equip the National Guard to make homeland security a primary mission.

Undertaking the Homeland Security Imperative

The nation must accept three facts of life after September 11. First, America is in a war against terrorists who want to attack its homeland, and it must act urgently to reduce its most serious vulnerabilities. Second, bolstering America's emergency preparedness in the near term is essential to minimizing casualties when an incident occurs on U.S. soil. Third, America's own ill-prepared response can do more damage to its citizens than any single attack by a terrorist. America is a powerful and resilient nation, and terrorists are not supermen. But the risk of self-inflicted harm to America's liberties and way of life is greatest during and immediately following a national trauma. Accordingly, preparing for the worst is an essential investment in preserving America at its best.

On September 11 we witnessed how warfare will likely be conducted against the United States for the foreseeable future. Prudence requires we assume America's adversaries, including Saddam Hussein, have learned from the attacks on the World Trade Center and the Pentagon, as well as the anthrax mailings, the extent to which the U.S. homeland is unprotected. They will also have observed that relatively low-cost terrorist operations directed at civilian targets can inflict extensive damage and profound disruption. In short, as long as catastrophic attacks are likely to yield tangible results in undermining America's economy and way of life, undertaking these attacks will be attractive to those who regard America as their enemy.

The Task Force identified several overarching considerations that should guide the nation's approach to homeland security.

Homeland security measures have deterrence value. U.S. counterterrorism initiatives abroad can be reinforced by making the U.S. homeland a less tempting target. We can transform the calculations of would-be terrorists by elevating the risk that (1) an attack on the United States will fail, and (2) the disruptive consequences of a successful attack will be minimal. It is especially critical that we bolster this deterrent now, since an inevitable consequence of the U.S. government's stepped-up military and diplomatic exertions will be to elevate the incentive to strike back before these efforts have their desired effect.

Federalism is a major asset. Given the size and complexity of the American society, there are no "one-size-fits-all" approaches to addressing the nation's most serious homeland vulnerabilities. Private-sector leaders and local authorities who are most familiar with those vulnerabilities will generally have the best insights on the most effective solutions. National coordination, resource support, and leadership by the federal government are all essential. But encouraging the capacity for states, localities, and the private sector to experiment and to be flexible in adapting to local and regional circumstances will ensure that our nation's approach to homeland security will be as dynamic as the threat that confronts us.

Domestic security measures must be pursued within an international context. The critical infrastructures that support the activities of our daily lives are linked to global networks. For example, the Northeast is dependent on electrical power generated in Quebec, and much of the natural gas used to fuel the power plants on the West Coast originates in the western provinces of Canada. Computer viruses such as the "Love Bug" know no boundaries as they cascade around the Internet at the speed of light. Many of the goods that fill America's stores originate from far-flung corners of the globe and arrive at U.S. borders in massive volumes via an extremely efficient and low-cost land, sea, and air transportation system. Efforts to protect these systems will fail unless they are pursued abroad as well as at home. The State Department, the Treasury Department, the Commerce Department, and the Office of the U.S. Trade Representative all have a critical role to play in making sure that our allies and trade partners work with us to ensure a collective approach to protecting critical infrastructures as we did with the year 2000 (Y2K) computer challenge.

Proceed with caution when embracing technological security "fixes." Technology can often serve as an enabler, but it must belong to a layered and dynamic system of defense that incorporates the contribution of human intuition and judgment. Any proposed technological "solution" must be evaluated against the costs and consequences if it should be compromised. In the end, security is not just about protecting American lives. It is also about sustaining systems that support our way of life in the face of designs to exploit or target those systems. This means that the security protocol must be able to manage any suspected or real terrorist breach without imposing costs so high as to compromise the very network it is designed to secure. Ultimately, the endgame must be to continue to live and prosper as an open, globally engaged society, not to become a nation trapped behind the modern versions of moats and castles.

Emergency preparedness can save lives—potentially a lot of lives. During the Cold War, the prevailing view among most Americans was that civil defense measures were futile—even self-defeating. Nuclear war was viewed as Armageddon, and preparations to survive a nuclear strike were seen as making nuclear war more probable because they eroded the presumed deterrence value of the "balance of terror." The contemporary security environment mandates that we put this anti-civil-defense bias behind us. America's ability to strike back with devastating force will not deter terrorists. Meanwhile a nuclear, chemical, or biological weapon poses a grave danger not only to those who are immediately exposed, but also to the entire emergency response and medical care system in the areas where such a weapon might be used. Heavy losses of seasoned firefighters, emergency technicians, police, and medical personnel can easily compromise a community's long-term capacity to provide for public health and safety.

A proactive mindset is key. The federal government is dedicating an extraordinary amount of energy and resources in response to the specific character of the September 11 attacks. Congress was quick to rush into law the Aviation and Transportation Security Act of 2001, which had the result of focusing the senior leadership in the U.S. Department of Transportation almost exclusively on hiring federal aviation passenger screeners and deploying new X-ray machines to the nation's airports. This kind of legislative response is understandable given the collective horror we shared in seeing hijacked commercial airliners used as missiles. Still, a reactive mindset is inevitably wasteful in terms of resources and can distract agencies from anticipating more probable future scenarios and from undertaking protective measures.

Homeland security measures will almost always have derivative benefits for other public and private goods. Terrorists may acquire a weapon of mass destruction, but they will not have unlimited access to these weapons. Consequently, they have to be selective about where, when, and how they will carry out an attack. No mayor or industry leader will want to be caught unprepared if his or her city or critical infrastructure is targeted. But making a case for investing in security safeguards for low probability–high consequence events can be a hard sell to a tax-wary populace or to CEOs under pressure to guard the bottom line.

Fortunately, many appropriate measures enacted to prevent and mitigate the consequences of a terrorist attack have other benefits. Bolstering the tools to detect and intercept terrorists will enhance the means authorities have to combat criminal acts such as cargo theft, violations of export controls, and narcotics and migrant smuggling. The tools used to save lives and property in the wake of a catastrophic terrorist act are largely the same as those that would be used in the event of a tragic industrial or transportation accident or natural disaster. As a result, some of the costs may be offset by reduced losses and lower insurance rates. Public health investments will inevitably provide the United States with more effective tools to manage the rising incidence of global diseases and pandemics. In short, sustaining support for actions to confront the new security environment may not be as difficult as it first appears because many of these measures can tangibly improve the quality of life in our society as well.

IDENTIFYING HOMELAND SECURITY IMPERATIVES

The Task Force recognizes that many useful initiatives are now underway that will advance homeland security. The case for establishing a new Department of Homeland Security is a compelling one, and legislation to create this department should be enacted without delay. The *National Strategy for Homeland Security* released by the White House on July 16, 2002, makes a salutary effort to frame this complex mission and to sketch out priorities. Equally commendable is the extent to which the strategy recognizes the importance of bolstering intelligence and warning systems, improving border and transportation security, enhancing domestic counterterrorism, protecting critical infrastructure and key assets, defending against catastrophic threats, and improving emergency preparedness and response.

In addition to reviewing the president's new strategy, the Task Force reviewed other recent contributions to the homeland security dialogue, most notably the National Academies' June 30, 2002, report, *Making the Nation Safer.*

In selecting the imperatives on which to focus, the Task Force decided to place its emphasis on issues that satisfied the following three criteria:

(1) the potential consequences of neglecting the imperative area are serious and well documented;

(2) the recommendations for addressing the imperative can be acted upon quickly; but

(3) these recommendations are not being pursued on an emergency basis.

The six critical mandates summarized above and detailed in the following sections represent only a portion of the homeland security agenda for our nation. There are other issues that we examined and judged to be very important, but we decided the measures to address them were adequate. For example, the president's Critical Infrastructure Protection Board—created in October 2001—recently released a draft *National Strategy to Secure Cyberspace* for public comment. This plan—developed by a private-public partnership involving representatives of corporations and nongovernmental organizations—outlines a comprehensive strategy to protect against the disruption of the complex, interdependent network of critical-infrastructure information systems that is essential to America's national and economic security.

Other issues require much more study before government actions should be taken on an expedited basis. For instance, preventive vaccinations of the general population against diseases such as smallpox may be harmful and even fatal for a small percentage of healthy people and are not presently an option for the millions of Americans with weakened immune systems. In short, the Task Force's list is inevitably an incomplete one. Nonetheless, the Task Force believes that acting on the critical issues targeted in this report with the kind of urgency our wartime footing mandates would contribute significantly to U.S. security in the months and years ahead. The nation's leaders in Washington, state capitals, counties, city halls, and boardrooms should be working overtime to address them—right now.

ISSUES AND RECOMMENDATIONS

1. TAP THE EYES AND EARS OF LOCAL AND STATE LAW ENFORCEMENT OFFICERS IN PREVENTING ATTACKS; MAKE FIRST RESPONDERS READY TO RESPOND.

Today, we are fighting a different kind of war—on two fronts. One front is Afghanistan, where we have the best technology, the best equipment, the best intelligence being sent right to the front, and no expense is spared. But for the first time in nearly 200 years, the second front is right

here at home. And to date, it's where we've seen the greatest loss of life. Yet we have insufficient equipment, too little training, and a lack of intelligence sharing with federal authorities.
—Martin O'Malley, Mayor of Baltimore, April 10, 2002

An estimated 8.5 million illegal aliens are living in the United States, including nearly 300,000 who have opted for life as fugitives rather than submitting to a final order of deportation. Stowaways arrive in U.S. ports and jump ship almost daily. These illegal migrants find it easy to blend in among the tens of millions of foreigners who arrive legally in the United States each year to travel, study, or work. Compounding the problem is widespread trafficking in forged or fraudulently obtained passports, licenses, and other identification documents. Baseline documents such as Social Security cards, birth certificates, and driver's licenses are particularly subject to abuse.

With just fifty-six field offices around the nation, the burden of identifying and intercepting terrorists in our midst is a task well beyond the scope of the Federal Bureau of Investigation (FBI). This burden could and should be shared with America's 650,000 local, county, and state law enforcement officers, but they clearly cannot lend a hand in a counterterrorism information void.

When it comes to combating terrorism, the police officers on the beat are effectively operating deaf, dumb, and blind. Terrorist watch lists provided by the U.S. Department of State to immigration and consular officials are still out of bounds for state and local police. In the interim period, as information-sharing issues get worked out, known terrorists will be free to move about to plan and execute their attacks. And if a catastrophic terrorist attack occurred today, emergency first responders—police, firefighters, and emergency medical personnel—in most of the nation's cities and counties are no better prepared to react now than they were prior to September 11. The tools of emergency preparedness are in very short supply. For instance, according to a survey done by the U.S. Conference of Mayors earlier this year:

- 79 percent of mayors reported a funding shortfall for necessary threat detection equipment, 77 percent for emergency response equipment, and 69 percent for personal protective apparel.
- 86 percent said they did not have adequate personal protective apparel and only 10 percent were satisfied with the protective equipment they had in the event of a biological attack.

Communications

In virtually every major city and county in the United States, no interoperable communications system exists to support police, fire departments, and county, state, regional, and federal response personnel during a major emergency. Radio frequencies are not available to support the post-incident communication demands that will be placed on them, and most cities have no redundant systems to use as backups. Portable radios will not work in high-rise buildings unless the buildings are equipped with repeater systems. Most U.S. cities have separate command-and-control functions for their police and fire departments, and little to no coordination exists between the two organizations. Furthermore, with few exceptions, first-responder commanders do not have access to secure radios, telephones, or video conferencing capabilities that can support communications with county, state, and federal emergency preparedness officials or National Guard leaders.

Protective gear

In the event of a chemical attack, a window of a few minutes to two hours exists to respond to the incident before morbidity and mortality rates skyrocket. Yet protective gear is often available only to a few specialized incident-response teams. Most communities will run short of even the most basic emergency response resources (e.g., lifesaving equipment, personal protection suits, oxygen, respirators, etc.) in six hours. Federal agency response teams can help but they will invariably arrive too late (i.e., no earlier than twelve hours after the attack).

Detection equipment
Portable and hand-held detection equipment for highly explosive, chemical, biological, and radiological materials is in short supply and notoriously unreliable in urban environments. Department of Defense and Department of Energy sensors deployed to local first responders have been issued without adequate personnel training on use and maintenance of the equipment, or guidance on what to do should the detection equipment register an alarm.

Training
Major field exercises are important tools for testing the adequacy of contingency plans, equipment, command-and-control procedures, and training. In all but America's largest cities, there is a paucity of resources and expertise to organize and conduct these large-scale exercises. For example, from 1996 to 1999, the federal government was able to provide WMD response training to only 134,000 of the nation's estimated 9 million first responders. Furthermore, only 2 percent of these 134,000 responders received hands-on training with live chemical agents. The Center for Domestic Preparedness in Anniston, Alabama, is the only facility in the nation where first responders can train with and gain first-hand knowledge of chemical agents. At peak capacity, it can train only 10,000 responders per year.

Recommendations
Our nation would not send its armed forces into harm's way without outfitting them with the right tools and skills. Our first responders and local law enforcement officers deserve the same investment—their lives and our lives depend on it. Therefore, the Task Force makes the following recommendations:
- Establish a twenty-four-hour operations center in each state that can provide a real time intergovernmental link between local and federal law enforcement. Field-level police would contact this center when they apprehend suspects to receive a red or green light to hold or release them based on a check of federal and Interpol databases.

- Step up efforts to rein in identity fraud by strengthening the anti-counterfeiting safeguards in state driver's licenses and passports, passing state laws criminalizing identity theft, and mobilizing 120-day joint local, state, and federal agency task forces to investigate and target phony-identification traffickers.
- Provide grants for states and cities to hire retired first responders on ninety-day renewable contracts to conduct comprehensive assessments on the status of urban emergency preparedness, including the state of protective gear, the adequacy of communications plans and equipment, and the availability of chemical antidotes.
- Fund the backlog of protective equipment and training requests by urban fire departments. This is a case where an immediate infusion of resources can make an immediate difference in reducing the risks to first responders and the morbidity and mortality of incident victims.
- Fund and deploy commercial off-the-shelf technologies that can integrate multiple radio platforms to support interoperable communications, including the ability to coordinate the flow of voice, image, and electronic information among responding agencies.
- Provide the national research labs with adequate funding to develop, field test, and widely distribute new portable and handheld sensor equipment suitable for urban environments.
- Ensure that the distribution of new technologies to first responders is supported by training and long-term maintenance contracts.
- Facilitate collaboration among the Federal Emergency Management Agency (FEMA), the National Guard, and state and local officials to deploy threat-based simulation models and training modules to support local emergency-operations-center training. WMD field exercises should be funded in all the nation's major urban areas over the next eighteen months. Senior police and fire officials from smaller cities and localities should be included in these exercises.

2. MAKE TRADE SECURITY A GLOBAL PRIORITY.

There is virtually no security for what is the primary system to transport global trade. The consequence of a terrorist incident using a container would be profound. … If terrorists used a sea container to conceal a weapon of mass destruction and detonated it on arrival at a port, the impact on global trade and the global economy could be immediate and devastating—all nations would be affected. No container ships would be allowed to unload at U.S. ports after such an event.

> —Robert Bonner, Commissioner, U.S. Customs Service,
> August 26, 2002

Immediately following the September 11 attacks, federal authorities ordered the closing of U.S. airspace to all flights, both foreign and domestic, shut down the nation's major seaports, and slowed truck, automobile, and pedestrian traffic across the land borders with Canada and Mexico to a trickle. Nineteen men wielding box cutters forced America to do to itself what no adversary could ever accomplish: a successful blockade of the United States. If a surprise terrorist attack were to happen tomorrow involving the sea, rail, or truck transportation systems that carry millions of tons of trade to the United States each day, the response would likely be the same—a self-imposed global embargo.

Vulnerable seaports

Ninety-five percent of all non–North American U.S. trade moves by sea and arrives in 361 ports around the nation. Despite the vital role seaports play in linking America to the world, both economically and militarily, port vulnerability studies for the nation's fifty largest ports are not scheduled to be completed for five more years. Over the past few decades, container traffic and energy imports increasingly have been concentrated in just a handful of ports, making them inviting targets. For instance, 43 percent of all the maritime containers that arrived in the United States in 2001 came through the ports of Los Angeles and Long Beach. As the recent West Coast port closures demonstrated, the cost to the economy of closing these ports totals approximately $1 billion per day for the first five days, rising exponentially thereafter. Nearly one-quarter of all of California's imported crude oil is offloaded in one geographically confined area. A USS *Cole*–style incident involving a ship offloading at that locale could leave Southern California without refined fuels within just a few days. The American Association of Port Authorities estimates the cost of adequate physical security at the nation's commercial seaports to be $2 billion. So far only $92.3 million in federal grants has been authorized and approved. Even then, the grants has not been awarded on the basis of a port's relative importance to the nation. The ports of Los Angeles and Long Beach requested $70 million in post–September 11 grants and were awarded just $6.175 million. The adequacy of such grant levels needs urgent reexamination.

Trade Dependence on the Intermodal Container
There are an estimated eleven million containers worldwide that are loaded and unloaded ten times per year. Ninety percent of the world's general cargo moves in these boxes. The architects of the intermodal revolution in transportation never considered security as a criterion—lower transport costs and improved speed and efficiency were the driving forces. For example, a new forty-foot container costs on average $2,500 to build and holds up to thirty tons of freight. The cost of the ocean voyage for a full container from Europe or Asia is approximately $1,500. There are no required security standards governing the loading or transport of an intermodal container. Most are "sealed" with a numbered lead tag that costs fifty cents.

If an explosive device were loaded in a container and set off in a port, it would almost automatically raise concern about the integrity of the 21,000 containers that arrive in U.S. ports each day and the many thousands more that arrive by truck and rail across U.S. land borders. A three-to-four-week closure of U.S. ports would bring the global container industry to its knees. Megaports such as Rotterdam and Singapore would have to close their gates to prevent boxes from piling up on their limited pier space. Trucks, trains, and barges would be stranded outside the terminals with no way to unload their boxes. Boxes bound for the United States would have to be unloaded from their outbound ships. Service contracts would need to be renegotiated. As this system became gridlocked, so would much of global commerce.

Trade Dependence on a Small Number of Border Crossings

The five major bridges and one tunnel that link Ontario to Michigan and New York account for 70 percent of all the trade between the United States and Canada—America's largest trading partner. The Ambassador Bridge between Detroit, Michigan, and Windsor, Ontario, alone carries $250 million per day, which is 27 percent of the total U.S.-Canada daily trade in merchandise. When these border crossings were effectively closed following the September 11 attacks, many of the "big three" automakers' assembly plants went idle within two days (the average assembly plant produces $1 million worth of automobiles per hour). Manufacturers and retailers depend on the unimpeded cross-border flow of trade to respond to "just-in-time" delivery imperatives. Despite this dependence, the U.S. and Canadian governments provide no security to these structures because they are either privately owned or controlled by binational bridge authorities. Since border inspections are done after vehicles cross the bridge or emerge from the tunnel, these inspections provide no protective value for these vital trade lines.

Recommendations

The Task Force makes the following recommendations:

- Develop a layered security system that focuses on the entire logistics and intermodal transportation network rather than on an unintegrated series of tactics aimed at addressing vulnerabilities at arrival ports or at already congested land borders.
- Develop standards for security at loading facilities for an intermodal container. Require certification of these standards and periodic independent audits for compliance as a condition for gaining access to an international transportation terminal.
- Identify and test commercial off-the-shelf sensors and tracking devices to assure in-transit visibility and accountability of container movements and conduct demonstration projects using volunteer commercial shippers to test their technological and commercial viability.

- Improve the accuracy, timing, and format for transmitting and sharing data about the contents, location, and chain of custody involving a container shipment.
- Accelerate the timetable for the action plans agreed to in the U.S.-Canada and U.S.-Mexico "smart-border" accords.
- Work with Canada to implement adequate security measures for cross-border bridges and the Detroit-Windsor tunnel.
- Task the U.S. Department of State, the U.S. Department of Commerce, and the Office of the U.S. Trade Representative with actively promoting rapid adoption of security standards governing surface and maritime transportation in bilateral and multilateral arrangements with America's trading partners. Work to advance these standards within appropriate international organizations such as the International Standards Organization, the International Maritime Organization, and the World Customs Organization. Retrofitting security into the global trade system is not only about mitigating the risk of terrorists' exploiting these systems to target the United States, but also about sustaining the system that underpins global commerce.

3. SET CRITICAL INFRASTRUCTURE PROTECTION PRIORITIES.

We are convinced that our vulnerabilities are increasing steadily, that the means to exploit those weaknesses are readily available and that the costs associated with an effective attack continue to drop. What is more, the investments required to improve the situation—now still relatively modest—will rise if we procrastinate.

—Report of the President's Commission on
Critical Infrastructure Protection, 1997

Our adversaries can attempt to strike anywhere, but their choice of target will likely not be indiscriminate. There are some targets in the United States that are of higher value than others in terms of visibility and disruptive potential. Not all critical infrastructure is equally critical. Decisions about what warrants the most immediate attention must be made on the basis of relative vulnerability and consequence. Many of the critical infrastructures that underpin our national economy and support our modern way of life remain as vulnerable to attack today as they were a year ago. In some instances, the U.S. government is just beginning the process of undertaking an initial inventory of these vulnerabilities. Greater attention has been paid to physical security—gates, guards, and guns—but few resources are focused on preparing to respond and restore critical systems should these protective measures fail. The Task Force reviewed the June 30, 2002, findings and recommendations contained within the National Academies' report, *Making the Nation Safer*. The areas that the Task Force finds most worrisome include the following:

Vulnerable Energy Distribution Systems

Crude oil must be refined and distributed if it is to be a meaningful source of energy. Power generation plants are worthless if the electricity cannot be transmitted to the factories, office buildings, and households that need it to power equipment and provide lighting and climate control. An adversary intent on disrupting America's reliance on energy need not target oil fields in the Middle East. The infrastructure for providing energy to end users is concentrated, sophisticated, and largely unprotected. Furthermore, some infrastructure lies offshore in the Gulf of Mexico, on the continental shelf, and within the territories of our North American neighbors.

Sixty percent of the Northeast's refined oil products are piped from refineries in Texas and Louisiana. A coordinated attack on several key pumping stations—most of which are in remote areas, are not staffed, and possess no intrusion-detection devices— could cause mass disruption to these flows. Nearly 50 percent of California's electrical supply comes from natural gas power plants, and 30 percent of California's natural gas comes from Canada. Compressor stations to maintain pressure cost up to $40 million each and are located every sixty miles on a pipeline. If these compressor stations were targeted, the pipeline would be shut down for an extended period of time. A coordinated attack on a selected set of key points in the electrical power system could result in multistate blackouts. While power might be restored in parts of the region within a matter of days or weeks, acute shortages could mandate rolling blackouts for as long as several years. Spare parts for critical components of the power grid are in short supply; in many cases they must be shipped from overseas sources.

Vulnerable Food and Water Supplies
The nation's food and agriculture industry represents a substantial sector of our economy and presents an inviting opportunity for biological attacks. As the recent foot-and-mouth disease outbreak among livestock in the United Kingdom illustrated, once a diagnosis of a contagious disease is made, the effect on domestic and export markets can be devastating. Similarly, there are vast numbers of pathogens that have the potential to wreak havoc on crops. Public anxieties over food contamination can undermine the demand for major foodstuffs for years. Yet, there is no equivalent to the Centers for Disease Control and Prevention (CDC) that could provide a shared communications network among states and the U.S. Department of Agriculture (USDA). Nor is there an effective means to communicate and coordinate internationally. Confusion over reporting obligations, who has jurisdiction, and to what extent they can provide adequate response to a potential attack promises to seriously compromise America's ability to contain the consequences of attacks on U.S. crops and livestock. For example, one recent exercise found that by the time the Agriculture Department's foreign-disease laboratory on Plum Island, N.Y., would have confirmed the first case of foot-and-mouth cross-border contamination, the disease would likely have spread to twenty-eight states.

The system that provides Americans with a basic element of life—water—remains vulnerable to mass disruption. Water systems are generally owned and maintained by local water companies and authorities that are slow to adopt new technologies and protocols. America's water supply is extremely vulnerable to contamination. This problem is compounded by the fact that extremely limited laboratory capacity and legal liability issues have made the routine monitoring of public water supplies for dangerous contaminants the exception rather than the rule. This lack of testing and monitoring capability can compound the consequences of a localized attack since there is no means to quickly reassure an anxious public across America that their drinking water is safe once a highly publicized incident takes place.

Vulnerable Clearinghouse Infrastructure to Support Financial Markets

Over the past two decades, the securities and banking industries have moved toward relying on a small number of core organizations for their post-trade clearing and settlement activities. If these systems were targeted by terrorists, the concentrated nature of these essential services could translate into profound disruption of daily economic life, both inside the United States and abroad. For example, clearing and settlement activities for the proper functioning of the government securities markets are essentially managed by just two banks, JP Morgan Chase and the Bank of New York. These two banks each extend approximately $1 trillion in 24-hour credit to their dealer and clearing customers each day. The sudden loss of these services could create a serious liquidity problem and likely damage public confidence in America's financial institutions and the systems upon which they borrow, invest, spend, and save.

Recommendations

The Task Force makes the following recommendations:
- Set critical infrastructure priorities by moving beyond a ranking of vulnerabilities within each sector. Instead, conduct a cross-sector analysis, placing a premium on addressing vulnerabilities that present the greatest risk of cascading disruption and losses across multiple sectors.
- Fund energy distribution vulnerability assessments to be completed in no more than six months.
- Fund a stockpile of modular backup components to quickly restore the operation of the energy grid should it be targeted.
- Work with Canada to put in place adequate security measures for cross-border pipelines.
- Bolster the capacity for the USDA to exercise control over detection and incidence management of plant and animal disease, drawing upon the best practices developed by the CDC for

managing human disease. Task the USDA with immediately bringing online a shared communications network to link it with states and U.S. trade partners.

- Provide adequate funding to significantly enhance the USDA's training in identifying foreign diseases and assume global leadership in devising a robust international system for monitoring the outbreak of animal and plant disease.
- Identify and remove legal liability constraints on routine testing of public water supplies for dangerous contaminants. Accelerate the development of adequate laboratory testing to serve local water companies and commissions.
- Create common integrated communication networks and realtime data and software backup repositories among the clearing banks, the Depository Trust and Clearing Corporation, dealers, and other key participants in the government securities market. Routinely test for recovery and resumption operations. The goal is to ensure that there are sufficient funds and securities available to market-makers in times of market stress so as to support the high level of liquidity required for trading.

4. BOLSTER PUBLIC HEALTH SYSTEMS.

Our concern is that bioterrorism preparedness funding must be adequate, lasting, and reliable to enable local public health agencies to build and sustain permanent improvements in their ability to protect their communities twenty-four hours a day, seven days a week. Most communities do not now have this level of protection.

—Thomas L. Milne, Executive Director,
National Association of County and
City Health Officials,
April 18, 2002

Agents used in biological attacks often require several days before victims start exhibiting acute symptoms. Early detection is key to stemming morbidity and mortality rates. Yet, with the possible exception of New York City, America's urban areas lack the advanced public health warning systems or specialized equipment to make this determination. There are simply not enough resources available within existing state and local budgets to remedy this situation in a timely way. Most local public health departments are barely funded and staffed to run during a normal 9 A.M. to 5 P.M. work week. Medical professionals often lack the training to properly diagnose and treat diseases spawned by biological agents. Many of the states' public health reporting systems are antiquated, slow, and outmoded. It can routinely take up to three weeks for a public health department to register a disease incident report in the national database. And there is no consensus on which language and diagnostic coding system should be used for a national database or how to safeguard that information.

Recent efforts in the federal government to respond to the bioterrorism threat may only add to confusion over responsibility and accountability. Responsibility for direction and coordination of public health efforts should rest with a substantially bolstered CDC with clear lines of communication to other departments and agencies such as the National Institutes of Health. Since much of the nation's research and most of its treatment capacity lie in the private sector, outreach is essential.

Chemical Versus Biological Attacks Have Different Imperatives
In chemical terrorism, detecting an attack is generally not a problem. People will show symptoms immediately: vomiting, suffering from seizures, experiencing respiratory distress, etc. The real challenge is deciphering which antidotes are appropriate and delivering them to the victims. The window of opportunity to mitigate the consequences of these attacks is very small—between a few minutes and two hours.

Detecting that there has been a biological attack can be far more problematic, since symptoms in a person do not show up right away. The window of opportunity for responding to the biological agent anthrax ranges from thirty-six to forty-eight hours and, for smallpox, nine to eleven days. For hemorrhagic fever viruses such as Ebola, an outbreak can occur from two to twenty-one days after the attack is launched. The problem of discerning the difference between flu-like symptoms and the onset of a deadly disease is compounded when physicians are unfamiliar with diagnosing and treating such diseases and, in any event, lack the medications to prescribe.

Little To No Capacity to Conduct Outbreak Investigations

Medical care providers who come in contact with victims are the first line of defense. Few of these professionals have received training on how to diagnose, treat, and report symptoms that are associated with a biological attack.

Most city and county public health agencies currently lack the resources to support emergency hotlines twenty-four hours a day. The National Association of City and County Health Officials estimates that localities need 10,000 to 15,000 new employees to work in public health preparedness functions. Given these shortages, few localities have the ability to assemble a team to conduct an outbreak investigation.

Public health laboratories cannot support a surge in the number of tests to verify the existence of a biological agent. Seven months after the anthrax mailings, there was a backlog of thousands of unexamined specimens suspected of being contaminated with anthrax powder around the United States.

Recommendations

The Task Force makes the following recommendations:

- Ensure that major cities and counties plan and train for truly catastrophic attacks. While these scenarios strike many as too horrific to contemplate, imagining and planning for them can potentially make the difference between a 20 percent casualty rate and an 80 percent or higher casualty rate.
- Make emergency federal funding available to address the highest-priority state, county, and city public health needs.
- Develop public health surveillance systems built around monitoring ambulance calls, pharmacies reporting an upsurge in the purchase of certain over-the-counter drugs, corporations and schools reporting a surge in worker or student absenteeism, and doctors and hospitals reporting an increase in walk-in patients.
- Develop and maintain call lists of retired nurses, doctors, and emergency medical technicians living in the community who

can be mobilized in an emergency. Provide annual training for these nonpracticing professionals and create a process for activating a "good Samaritan" clause to override malpractice issues.

- Identify and maintain call lists of knowledgeable experts who can authoritatively speak to the media about nuclear, chemical, or biological agents, symptoms of exposures, and recommended safeguards. Develop communications strategies and prepare educational materials and media guides for radio and TV on survival fundamentals for attacks involving WMD.
- Recruit major corporations and schools to help provide medications during an emergency. While the federal government will soon have the capability to ship antibiotics and vaccines from the twelve national pharmaceutical stockpiles to urban areas within six hours, there are currently no local distribution plans to get these medicines to the general population.
- Provide funding to hospitals to pre-wire and outfit certain common areas such as lobbies, cafeterias, and hallways to support a surge in patients. Negotiate arrangements with hotels and conference centers to provide bed space for spillover patients.

5. REMOVE FEDERAL GOVERNMENT OBSTACLES TO PARTNERING.

Obstacles for using our most potent resources for countering catastrophic terrorism must be identified and overcome.

—Committee on Science and Technology for Countering Terrorism, National Research Council, June 30, 2002

The burden of preparing and responding to catastrophic terrorist attacks lies primarily outside the federal government at the local and state levels and with the private-sector companies that own and operate much of the nation's critical infrastructure. Most of the expertise about both the vulnerabilities and the most practical protective measures to save lives and avert mass societal and economic disruption rests at this level as well. The federal government must provide leadership by issuing the call to action, supporting forums convened to address these issues, and supplying as much specific information as possible to key decision-makers on the nature of the threat.

Engaging the Private Sector

The barriers to greater information-sharing between the public and private sectors are not simply bureaucratic and cultural. Private-sector leaders have legal concerns with respect to liability. They also worry about violating antitrust laws and are apprehensive that sensitive security information may be publicly disclosed by way of FOIA. For their part, government agencies find it almost impossible to discuss matters that may involve classified security information. Protecting the public's right to know and ensuring free and competitive markets are cornerstones of our democracy. Safeguarding classified material is essential to protecting sources and methods. As a practical matter, however, the current rules confound the ability of the private sector to share information with public authorities on vulnerabilities within critical infrastructure, and preclude the ability of federal government officials to share anything but the most generic security and threat information.

The real value of sharing information is that it can encourage efforts to develop innovative security measures that involve all the relevant stakeholders. But innovation also generally requires the infusion of federal resources to support research and development. Here the sense of urgency required by the homeland security mission collides with the lethargic and arcane system governing federal procurement—the federal acquisition rules. These rules, which run literally into the thousands of pages, may be tolerable for routine government purchases, but without a more streamlined process to move federal resources, change will be measured in terms of years, not in the weeks and months that taking emergency measures to address our most serious vulnerabilities requires. Also, private companies that agree to work with the public sector to assist in developing and providing security measures will require legal safeguards that appropriately reduce their liability exposure. Good faith efforts to advance security should not result in a risk of bankruptcy or huge litigation costs should these measures ultimately fail to deter or prevent terrorist attacks.

Tap International Expertise

While terrorism may be a new and painful experience for most Americans, regrettably many American allies such as the United Kingdom, France, Spain, and Israel have been confronted by this challenge for some time. Countries such as Switzerland provide a model for how civil defense efforts can be coordinated and largely resourced at the national level and adapted and managed at the local level. The United States does not have a monopoly on insight and ingenuity. It should be keen to learn from others' experience by sending research teams abroad to identify the best practices that could be implemented quickly here in the United States.

Recommendations

The Task Force makes the following recommendations:

- Draw on private-sector experts who are involved in the design and operations of critical infrastructures such as the electric-power grid, telecommunications, gas and oil, banking and finance, transportation, water supply, public health services, and emergency services. Enlist their participation to conduct government-sponsored vulnerability assessments and to participate in red-team activities.
- Enact an "Omnibus Anti–Red Tape" law with a two-year sunset clause for approved private-public homeland security task forces to include (1) a fast-track security clearance process that permits the sharing of "secret-level" classified information with non-federal and industry leaders; (2) a FOIA exemption in instances when leaders in critical infrastructure industries agree to share information about their security vulnerabilities with federal agencies; (3) exemption of private participants in these task forces from antitrust rules; (4) permitting homeland security appropriations to be managed under the more liberal rules governing research and development programs in the Department of Defense rather than according to the customary federal acquisition rules; and (5) liability of safeguards and limits.
- Fund and deploy survey teams in the United Kingdom, France, Spain, and Israel to conduct studies on managing urban

terrorism, evaluating European airline security procedures, and examining private-public intelligence-sharing arrangements.

6. FUND, TRAIN, AND EQUIP THE NATIONAL GUARD TO MAKE HOMELAND SECURITY A PRIMARY MISSION.

The National Guard will play a critical role when the next catastrophic terrorist attack happens on American soil, and it must be well trained and equipped. Governors will expect National Guard units in their states to help with detecting chemical and biological agents, treating the victims, managing secondary consequences, and maintaining civil order. The National Guard has highly disciplined personnel spread throughout the nation in 5,475 units. The men and women who make up its ranks often come from the local community in which their unit is based. When called up by governors, the National Guard can be used to enforce civil laws—unlike regular military forces which are bound by *posse comitatus* restrictions on performing law enforcement duties. The National Guard's medical units, engineer units, military police units, and ground and air transport units will likely prove indispensable in helping to manage the consequences of a terrorist attack.

Adapting to the New Homeland and Security Imperative
Governors, charged with developing state homeland security plans, will look to their National Guard units to fulfill such needs as
- State-of-the-art communications systems necessary for command-and-control during the chaos of a terrorist attack;
- Personnel in order to evacuate, quarantine, and protect residents as need be;
- Knowledge of chemical, biological, and radiological attacks and the capability to respond to them;
- The capacity to provide local medical centers with additional trauma and triage capabilities.

The National Guard is currently equipped and trained primarily for carrying out its role in supporting conventional combat units overseas. The homeland security mission can draw on many of these capabilities but requires added emphasis on

- Responding to a biological attack—the National Guard's focus in recent years has been primarily on surviving and fighting in a battlefield where chemical weapons have been deployed.
- Acquiring protection, detection, and other equipment that is tailored for complex urban environments.
- Training to provide civil support in the aftermath of a large-scale catastrophic attack.

Recommendations

An aggressive approach to revamping the capabilities of National Guard units designated to respond to domestic terrorist attacks can in the short term provide a more robust response capability while states and localities work to bring their individual response mechanisms up to par. In order for the National Guard to fulfill this mission, the Task Force recommends the following:

- Congress should authorize and fund additional training for National Guard units to work with state civil authorities and to conduct exercises with local first responders in support of the new homeland security plans being developed by each governor.
- Triple the number of WMD–Civil Support Teams from twenty-two to sixty-six, develop capabilities so that response times are reduced to within the narrow window in which their presence is still valuable, and reevaluate equipment and training programs in order to develop response capabilities for the full range of WMD threats in urban environments.
- Bolster the National Guard's "train the trainers" programs to quickly bring baseline training on recognizing and responding to WMD events to localities around the country.
- Move away from using National Guard resources where their deployment has a minimal impact. National Guardsmen are too valuable to be assigned to borders and airports where they

are limited in the functions they can perform. Instead, the agencies with the mandate in these areas need to be given the necessary resources to perform their missions without National Guard help.

• Redress the pay and job-protection discrepancies between when National Guard units are called up by the president and when they are called up by a governor. When governors order an activation, guardsmen receive no protection that allows them to return to their civilian jobs as provided under the Soldiers and Sailors Civil Relief Act. In addition, when on state active duty they may be paid as little as $75 a day.

Conclusion

Quickly mobilizing the nation to prepare for the worst is an act of prudence, not fatalism. In the twenty-first century, security and liberty are inseparable. The absence of adequate security elevates the risk that laws passed immediately in the wake of surprise terrorist attacks will be reactive, not deliberative. Predictably, the consequence will be to compound the initial harm incurred by a tragic event with measures that overreach in terms of imposing costly new security mandates and the assumption of new government authorities that may erode our freedoms. Accordingly, aggressively pursuing America's homeland security imperatives immediately may well be the most important thing we can do to sustain our cherished freedoms for future generations.

Preparedness at home also plays a critical role in combating terrorism by reducing its appeal as an effective means of warfare. Acts of catastrophic terrorism produce not only deaths and physical destruction but also societal and economic disruption. Thus, as important as it is to try and attack terrorist organizations overseas and isolate those who support them, it is equally important to eliminate the incentive for undertaking these acts in the first place. If the disruptive effects of terrorism can be sharply reduced, if not eliminated, America's adversaries may be deterred from taking their battles to the streets of our nation's homeland.

TASK FORCE MEMBERS

CHARLES G. BOYD is Chief Executive Officer and President of Business Executives for National Security (BENS). Before retiring from the U.S. Air Force in August 1995, General Boyd served as Deputy Commander in Chief for the U.S. European Command.

WARREN CHRISTOPHER is a Senior Partner at O'Melveny & Myers. He served as Secretary of State from January 1993 to January 1997 under President Bill Clinton.

WILLIAM J. CROWE is a Senior Adviser at Global Options. Previously, Admiral Crowe served as the Chairman of the Joint Chiefs of Staff under Ronald Reagan.

STEPHEN E. FLYNN, who directed the Task Force, is the Jeane J. Kirkpatrick Senior Fellow for National Security Studies at the Council on Foreign Relations and recently retired as a Commander in the U.S. Coast Guard. He served in the White House Military Office during the first Bush administration and as a Director for Global Issues on the National Security Council staff during the Clinton administration.

STEPHEN FRIEDMAN is a Senior Principal at Marsh & McLennan Capital. He is a retired Chairman of Goldman, Sachs & Company.

GARY HART, who co-chaired the Task Force, has been Of Counsel with Coudert Brothers since 1994. As Senator from Colorado from 1975 to 1987, he served on the Armed Services, Budget, and Environment Committees and was also a Congressional Adviser to the second round of Strategic Arms Limitation Talks (SALT II) in Geneva.

Note: Institutional affiliations are for identification purposes only.

JAMES K. KALLSTROM is Senior Executive Vice President at MBNA America Bank. After September 11, 2001, Mr. Kallstrom took a leave of absence from MBNA America and served as the Director of the Office of Public Security for the State of New York.

JOSHUA LEDERBERG is a Nobel laureate and serves as President Emeritus and Sackler Foundation Scholar at Rockefeller University.

DONALD B. MARRON is Chairman of UBS America and Managing General Partner of Lightyear Capital. Previously, he served for twenty years as Chairman and CEO of Paine Webber Group, Inc., until its merger with UBS in 2000.

PHILIP A. ODEEN is Chairman of TRW Inc. Before joining TRW Inc., Mr. Odeen was President of BDM International, Inc., and a Vice Chairman at Coopers & Lybrand LLP.

WARREN B. RUDMAN, who co-chaired the Task Force, is currently a Partner in the international law firm Paul, Weiss, Rifkind, Wharton and Garrison and formerly Chairman of the President's Foreign Intelligence Advisory Board under President Clinton. He represented New Hampshire in the U.S. Senate from 1980 to 1992.

GEORGE P. SHULTZ is the Thomas W. and Susan B. Ford Distinguished Fellow at the Hoover Institution. He has served as Secretary of State, Secretary of the Treasury, Secretary of Labor, and Director of the Office of Management and Budget.

ANNE-MARIE SLAUGHTER is Dean of the Woodrow Wilson School of Public and International Affairs at Princeton University. Prior to her appointment at Princeton, she was the J. Sinclair Armstrong Professor of International, Foreign, and Comparative Law at Harvard Law School.

HAROLD E. VARMUS is President and Chief Executive Officer of Memorial Sloan-Kettering Cancer Center and a Nobel laureate in physiology/medicine. Previously, he served as Director of the National Institutes of Health.

Task Force Members

JOHN W. VESSEY is Chairman of the Center for Preventive Action at the Council on Foreign Relations and previously served as Chairman of the Joint Chiefs of Staff as well as Vice Chief of Staff of the U.S. Army.

WILLIAM H. WEBSTER is a Partner at the law firm of Milbank, Tweed, Hadley & McCloy. He served as Director of Central Intelligence from 1987 to 1991 and as Director of the Federal Bureau of Investigation from 1978 to 1987.

STEVEN WEINBERG is Director of the Theory Group of the University of Texas. He is a Nobel laureate in physics and a recipient of the National Medal of Science.

Note: Institutional affiliations are for identification purposes only.

OTHER REPORTS OF INDEPENDENT TASK FORCES SPONSORED BY THE COUNCIL ON FOREIGN RELATIONS

*†*Threats to Democracy* (2002)
  Madeleine K. Albright and Bronislaw Geremek, Co-Chairs; Morton H.
  Halperin, Project Director; Elizabeth Frawley Bagley, Associate Director

*†*Balkans 2010* (2002)
  Edward C. Meyer, Chair; William L. Nash, Project Director

*†*Terrorist Financing* (2002)
  Maurice R. Greenberg, Chair; William F. Wechsler and Lee S. Wolosky,
  Project Co-Directors

*†*Enhancing U.S. Leadership at the United Nations* (2002)
  David Dreier and Lee H. Hamilton, Co-Chairs; Lee Feinstein and Adrian
  Karatnycky, Project Co-Directors; Cosponsored with Freedom House

*†*Testing North Korea: The Next Stage in U.S. and ROK Policy* (2001)
  Morton I. Abramowitz and James T. Laney, Co-Chairs; Robert A. Manning,
  Project Director

*†*The United States and Southeast Asia: A Policy Agenda for the New
  Administration* (2001)
  J. Robert Kerrey, Chair; Robert A. Manning, Project Director

*†*Strategic Energy Policy: Challenges for the 21st Century* (2001)
  Edward L. Morse, Chair; Amy Myers Jaffe, Project Director

*†*State Department Reform* (2001)
  Frank C. Carlucci, Chair; Ian J. Brzezinski, Project Coordinator;
  Cosponsored with the Center for Strategic and International Studies

*†*U.S.-Cuban Relations in the 21st Century: A Follow-on Report* (2001)
  Bernard W. Aronson and William D. Rogers, Co-Chairs; Julia Sweig and
  Walter Mead, Project Directors

*†*A Letter to the President and a Memorandum on U.S. Policy Toward Brazil*
  (2001)
  Stephen Robert, Chair; Kenneth Maxwell, Project Director

*†*Toward Greater Peace and Security in Colombia* (2000)
  Bob Graham and Brent Scowcroft, Co-Chairs; Michael Shifter, Project
  Director; Cosponsored with the Inter-American Dialogue

†*Future Directions for U.S. Economic Policy Toward Japan* (2000)
  Laura D'Andrea Tyson, Chair; M. Diana Helweg Newton, Project Director

*†*Promoting Sustainable Economies in the Balkans* (2000)
  Steven Rattner, Chair; Michael B.G. Froman, Project Director

*†*Nonlethal Technologies: Progress and Prospects* (1999)
  Richard L. Garwin, Chair; W. Montague Winfield, Project Director

*†*U.S. Policy Toward North Korea: Next Steps* (1999)
  Morton I. Abramowitz and James T. Laney, Co-Chairs; Michael J. Green,
  Project Director

†*Safeguarding Prosperity in a Global Financial System: The Future Interna-
  tional Financial Architecture* (1999)
  Carla A. Hills and Peter G. Peterson, Co-Chairs; Morris Goldstein, Project
  Director

* *Strengthening Palestinian Public Institutions* (1999)
  Michael Rocard, Chair; Henry Siegman, Project Director

*†*U.S. Policy Toward Northeastern Europe* (1999)
  Zbigniew Brzezinski, Chair; F. Stephen Larrabee, Project Director

*†*The Future of Transatlantic Relations* (1999)
  Robert D. Blackwill, Chair and Project Director

*†*U.S.-Cuban Relations in the 21st Century* (1999)
  Bernard W. Aronson and William D. Rogers, Co-Chairs; Walter Russell
  Mead, Project Director

---

†Available on the Council on Foreign Relations website at http://www.cfr.org.
*Available from Brookings Institution Press. To order, call 1-800-275-1447.